ANIMAL SAFARI

Anteaters

by Megan Borgert-Spaniol

BLASTOFF! READERS

BELLWETHER MEDIA · MINNEAPOLIS, MN

Note to Librarians, Teachers, and Parents:

Blastoff! Readers are carefully developed by literacy experts and combine standards-based content with developmentally appropriate text.

Level 1 provides the most support through repetition of high-frequency words, light text, predictable sentence patterns, and strong visual support.

Level 2 offers early readers a bit more challenge through varied simple sentences, increased text load, and less repetition of high-frequency words.

Level 3 advances early-fluent readers toward fluency through increased text and concept load, less reliance on visuals, longer sentences, and more literary language.

Level 4 builds reading stamina by providing more text per page, increased use of punctuation, greater variation in sentence patterns, and increasingly challenging vocabulary.

Level 5 encourages children to move from "learning to read" to "reading to learn" by providing even more text, varied writing styles, and less familiar topics.

Whichever book is right for your reader, Blastoff! Readers are the perfect books to build confidence and encourage a love of reading that will last a lifetime!

This edition first published in 2012 by Bellwether Media, Inc.

No part of this publication may be reproduced in whole or in part without written permission of the publisher. For information regarding permission, write to Bellwether Media, Inc., Attention: Permissions Department, 5357 Penn Avenue South, Minneapolis, MN 55419.

Library of Congress Cataloging-in-Publication Data

Borgert-Spaniol, Megan, 1989-
Anteaters / by Megan Borgert-Spaniol.
   p. cm. – (Blastoff! Readers. Animal safari)
Includes bibliographical references and index.
 Summary: "Developed by literacy experts for students in kindergarten through grade three, this book introduces anteaters to young readers through leveled text and related photos"–Provided by publisher.
ISBN 978-1-60014-714-2 (hardcover : alk. paper)
1. Myrmecophagidae–Juvenile literature. I. Title.
QL737.E24B67 2012
599.3'14–dc23   2011028864

Printed in the United States of America, North Mankato, MN.

010112   1207

Contents

What Are Anteaters?

Anteaters are **mammals** with long **snouts**. They have thick hair that feels like straw.

Anteaters have long, bushy tails. They curl up under their tails when they sleep.

Where Anteaters Live

Anteaters live in **swamps**, grasslands, and forests.

Finding Food

Anteaters use their sharp **claws** to find food. They make holes in anthills and **termite** mounds.

Then they stick
their tongues
inside the holes to
grab the **insects**.

Anteaters stand on their back legs to face jaguars and pumas. Their strong tails help them **balance**.

They roar and
show their claws
to scare these
predators away.

Pups

Baby anteaters
are called pups.
They live with their
mothers for about
two years.

A pup rides
around on its
mother's back.
Hang on, pup!

Glossary

balance—to stay steady and not fall

claws—sharp, curved nails at the end of an animal's fingers and toes

insects—small animals with six legs and hard outer bodies; insect bodies are divided into three parts.

mammals—warm-blooded animals that have backbones and feed their young milk

predators—animals that hunt other animals for food

snouts—the jaws and noses of some animals

swamps—land areas that are partly covered with water for most of the year

termite—an insect that feeds on wood

To Learn More

AT THE LIBRARY

Antill, Sara. *Giant Anteater*. New York, N.Y.: Windmill Books, 2011.

Bentley, Dawn. *The Icky Sticky Anteater*. Santa Monica, Calif.: Piggy Toes Press, 2000.

Waber, Bernard. *An Anteater Named Arthur*. Boston, Mass.: Houghton Mifflin, 1967.

ON THE WEB

Learning more about anteaters is as easy as 1, 2, 3.

1. Go to www.factsurfer.com.

2. Enter "anteaters" into the search box.

3. Click the "Surf" button and you will see a list of related Web sites.

With factsurfer.com, finding more information is just a click away.

Index

The images in this book are reproduced through the courtesy of: Henry Wilson, front cover, p. 9 (right); SA TEAM / FOTO NATURA / MINDEN PIC / National Geographic Stock, p. 5; Morales Morales / Photolibrary, p. 7; Gary Cook / Alamy, p. 9 (top); Johannes Compaan, p. 9 (left); jspix jspix / Photolibrary, p. 11; Michel & Christine Denis-Huot / Biosphoto, p. 13; LUCIANO CANDISANI / MINDEN PICTURES / National Geographic Stock, p. 15; Luiz C. Marigo / Photolibrary, p. 17; ZSSD / Minden Pictures, p. 19; Juniors Bildarchiv / Alamy, p. 21.